Life in Kentucky and More

Life in Kentucky and more

Neda Brewer

ISBN:	Softcover	978-1-5144-1149-0
	eBook	978-1-5144-1148-3

Print information available on the last page.

Rev. date: 01/13/2016

To order additional copies of this book, contact:
Xlibris
1-888-795-4274
www.Xlibris.com
Orders@Xlibris.com
722962

Contents

DEDICATION

I have to dedicate this book to my friends, who encouraged me to put my thoughts,on paper. I also dedicate it to my children and grandchildren. My granddaughter Tori, whom I consider a great writer, and my grandsons, Justin, Max, Christian, and Nicholas. My youngest granddaughter Emma, who helped me write a humorous poem.

Special dedication to me deceased husband Terry. The unfortunate accident that took his life, gave me the idea to put my thoughts in poetry. I have humorous, sad and life experiences. My poetry depends on my mood I'm in.

A WALK DOWN MEMORY LANE

I'm going for a walk today,
Down the path called Memory lane.
to see if there's any way of finding
the place from which I came.
I can visit the place called, Contentment,
I'll linger there for a while.
It's warm, and so inviting,
The memories, bring on a smile.
Then I will try to visit, Resentment,
It's dark, and gloomy, and cold.
There's shadows that surround you,
They follow, everywhere you go.
On my way back to Memory Lane,
I'll stop at a place called Hope,
There's laughter and joy and happy tears,
And friends who help carry the load.
All in all, it will be a great trip,
When I return, I can be at peace,
My soul can be at rest now,
My travels, will be complete.

A COAL MINER'S THOUGHTS

I often wonder, about the coal miner,
When he enters that deep dark hole.
Does he forget to say a silent prayer?
Does he ask God to save his soul?
Is he scared he may not make it back out
To his family, that's waiting at home.
Does he think about how they would survive,
If suddenly, they are left all alone
Is he complaining about working in the low coal?
And the scars, and scabs that he wears.
I believe the coal miner, is very brave,
He's fulfilling the responsibility, he bears.
Many a coal miner has lost his life,
In that dark, and damp tomb underground.
My only prayer is that they knew Jesus,
Then peace in Heaven will be found.

A House Is Not A Home

A House is not a home, it's just a shell.
A hug from someone you love,
Can make your heart swell.
Material things, are not important,
Except, the pictures on the wall.
Without someone inside to love you
It won't feel like home, at all.
It makes no difference, if it's a
mansion, or a castle on a hill,
You won't really be happy,
You life can't be fulfilled.
To turn that shell, into a home,
Find a partner, to share your life,
The shell will be a home at last.
With togetherness and warmth inside.

A MESSAGE TO JESUS

Happy birthday to you Jesus.
Thank you for all you have done.
I just wanted to ask a question,
Could you give a message, to my loved ones?
Tell mom and dad, I said, thank you,
For the Christmas's we shared.
Let them know it didn't matter,
If sometimes the tree, was bare.
I know they did the best they could.
To make our Christmas's bright,
We still had food on the table,
Jesus, tell them it was alright.
Tell all my brothers, and sisters,
I remember them every year,
They're better off, with you now,
I don't have to shed as many tears.
Thank you Jesus, once again,
Without you I would be lost.
You gave the greatest gift, of all.
When you were nailed to the cross.

A New Spin On Nursery Rhymes

Peter Peter pumpkin eater
He supposedly had a wife
But I would guess
She didn't stay long
She got tired of pumpkin pies

Hey diddle diddle
The cat and the fiddle
The cow jumped over the moon
If thats the truth
I'll buy a cow
And go to Mars real soon

Little Jack Horner
Sat in a corner
Eating his Christmas pie
His sister wanted some
But he said no
And made the poor thing cry

Humpty Dumpty sat on a wall
No wonder he fell down
It's hard to sit anywhere
When your little bottom is round

A NEW SPIN ON NURSERY RHYMES 2

Mary had a little lamb
It's fleece was white as snow
That's because she scrubbed it hard
With bleach and Ivory soap

Jack be nimble
Jack be quick
That's the way the story goes
He wasn't very quick at all
Because he burned his little toes

Mary Mary quite contrary
How does your garden grow
With morning glories
And lots of weeds
By neglecting the garden hoe

Old Mother Hubbard
Went to the cupboard
To get her poor dog a bone
She said "I only have one"
But I'm making soup
So you, poor dog, can have none

A NEW SPIN ON NURSERY RHYMES 3

The three little kittens
They lost their mittens
That's the way the limerick goes
But what good is two mittens
When each little kitten
Has a total of sixteen toes

Pat-a-cake Pat-a-cake bakers man
Make me a cake as fast as you can
I've got a sweet tooth
And my sugar is dropping
Hurry up please
Don't worry about the topping
But please don't pat it
I'm scared of germs
You may not like it
But those are my terms

Little Miss Muffet
Sat on a tuffet
Eating her curds and whey
She said "This is crazy'
I want biscuits and gravy
She threw her curds and whey,away!

A New Spin On Nursery Rhymes 4

Rub-a-dub-dub
Three men in a tub
Was there a shortage of water
They should have took turns
Didn't they know
Nothing could look much odder

Little Bo Peep
Got tired of her sheep
And said that they were lost
If the truth be known
She sold them all
She got tired of all the baa's

Jack and Jill
Went up the hill
Supposedly to get water
But Jill's mama didn't believe that tale
So she went up the hill and got her

A Soldiers Prayer

When a soldier goes off to fight a war,
His family he leaves behind.
He has no way of knowing,
If he's seen them for the last time.
He's a dedicated and brave soldier,
Fighting for his fellow man.
Fighting to save his country,
To restore peace to the land.
I try to imagine the prayer he is saying
As the planes are flying low,
Dear God please wrap your arm around me,
Don't let my strength, and courage go.
My wife and children, are waiting for me,
Please God, let me make it safely home.
Lord I am but a simple man,
I'm fighting to keep my country free.
Death does not frighten me Lord,
If I die, I'll do it victoriously.
I love my wife, I love my children,
I'm no better than any man.
I beg of you Lord, please spare me,
so I can make it back to family again.

A STRANGER CAME TO CALL

With a voice like Clark Gable,
He wooed me with his charm.
He wanted to come to see me,
I thought,so whats the harm?
I said okay, the plans were made,
We set a date to meet.
The day arrived, my hands were shaky,
I said to myself, don't get cold feet!
Be still my heart, I just can't take it,
I've never felt this way before.
My palms were sweating, my heart
was pounding, there came a knock
at my front door.
I opened the door,I took a look,
And there standing in front of me,
Was a man who looked like Gomer Pyle,
My Clark Gable wasn't meant to be.
I invited him in, we chatted for awhile
I made excuses for him to leave.
Needless to say, I'm back to square one
I'm still looking for my handsome dream.
The time is fleeting, I have to hurry,
My clock is running out of time.
I hope to meet,a tall dark stranger,
And maybe soon, I can call him mine.

All I Need Is Love

Give me a humble cottage,
With clothes from the cheapest store.
As long as I have love at home,
Could I ask for anything more?
You can have your million dollar mansion,
You can wear your designer clothes,
Just give me a wonderful soulmate,
With just a single red rose.
What good is all the fortune,
When you are lying alone at night.
Sometimes the only things we need,
Are two arms, to hold us tight.
All I have ever wanted in life,
is peace, and joy and love,
we can't take fame and fortune,
To the real mansion, in heaven above.

AMAZING KENTUCKY

Kentucky, is such a beautiful state
With mountains so tall, the sun rise is late.
The grass is a lovely shade of blue.
The wildflowers create a breathtaking view.
Where everyone talks with a southern drawl,
Like, Howdy Folks, and come Back y''all
Making a living, is hard at times,
The work is dwindling, in the Kentucky coalmine.
I wouldn't trade my heritage, for all the gold.
We never knew, we were just Po' folks.
You can take the girl, out of the hills,
I'm proud to say, I'm a country hick still.

An Old Fashioned Christmas

Let us have an old fashioned Christmas
With a tree cut fresh from the woods.
Homemade garlands, wrapped around the tree,
And pine wreaths, that smell so good.
A big tin foil heart, to signify the night,
In Palestine, on a night, so serene,
the whole sky glowed with a blinding light,
The brightest star, ever to be seen.
That night, in a cold and lonely stable,
Our Savior, Jesus Christ was born.
let us tell the story, around the Christmas tree,
As we celebrate, the birth, of our Lord.
The smell of the turkey, roasting in the oven,
Homemade cake and delicious pumpkin pies,
It will be the greatest Christmas,
As we eat,by the candle light.
Christmas is for,all little children,
their innocense,is worth more than gold.
have a wonderful,and joyous holiday,
As we celebrate,in the days of old.

APPALACHIAN BEAUTY

In the Appalachian mountains,
It's a beautiful scene,
Before all the trees have turned to green.
You can see for miles, and mile away,
Walking the trails, on a clear sunny day.
The Appalachians, have many wonders to behold,
The mountain peaks, and the valleys below.
I can sit for hours, and admire the view.
In the early morning, when the fog rolls through.
Then springtime comes, with a beauty unseen,
The flowers are blooming, the trees turn green.
Spring or summer, winter or fall,
There's a beauty in the seasons,
I love them all.

ARE YOU GOING HOME FOR CHRISTMAS

Are you going home for Christmas?
For a visit, with mom and dad,
Going home to show you love them,
There may be a time, you will wish you had.
The years go by so swiftly,
Before you know it, they'll be gone.
Christmas won't feel the same anymore,
Please try to make it home.
if you have become a mom or dad,
Just imagine how life would be,
If suddenly your children aren't with you,
To share the warmth of the Christmas tree.
It isn't about the presents we get,
Or the food we all will share.
It's about spending time together,
To show each other, how much we care.
Most important, it's the day our Savoir was born,
In a cold stable, on a bed of hay.
Take time out to celebrate the reason,
We come together, on this special day.

ARROWHEADS

I love digging arrowheads,
It's a thrill, like no other.
At times I dig, and dig, and dig,
They're really hard to uncover.
I don't worry about the hot sun,
My only interest is finding,
Just one more precious arrowhead,
As the day is slowly unwinding.
It's really sad to think about,
The hard life Indians had to live,
I cherish everyone I find,
It's the white man Indians had to forgive.
Each time I find another one,
I wonder about it's history,
How did they chisel them so well,
To me it's still a mystery.
I'm proud to say I have Cherokee blood,
From both of my grandmothers,
I think that's why I feel so proud,
When another arrowhead, I uncover.

As I'm Lying All Alone

I can almost, hear the sounds, of my
old Kentucky home,
as I'm lying in the bed at night, and
I'm feeling all alone.
I can hear the sounds of laughter,
As we talked, by the fireside.
Where did time go, so swiftly,
I ask out loud, it doesn't seem right.
I miss the smiles of mom and dad,
And the lectures, when we would fight.
All the things we shared as family
Comes to my mind when i can't sleep.
I may not have my family now,
But the precious memories, I can keep.
One day we will have a reunion,
Like we have never had before
All of our family will be together
When we enter heaven's door

BLACKEY KENTUCKY

Eastern Kentucky,is the place I call home,
It makes no difference, how long I've been gone.
I still get excited, to go back and see,
The little town, of Blackey Kentucky.
it's changed a lot, some buildings are gone,
To me it will always, be my home.
The church I attended, as a child is still there.
The old blue bridge isn't going anywhere.
I would love to be able to visit the store,
Run by Joe Begley, but he's not there anymore.
There's a lot of memories, I have of this town.
The old railroad houses, have been torn down.
Doc Adams's office and the school on the hill.
The old railroad depot, I remember them still.
It's just melancholy, memories for me,
And as they say, what will be, will be.

BRENDA

I got a call from my sister today.
It broke my heart,with what she had to say.
The doctor had given her some really bad news.
She was crying hard, and I knew it was true.
Brenda never let anything make her scared.
This time was different,from the words she had heard.
I pray for God to make her well,
I need her here, because she never fails,
To make me laugh, when I'm feeling down.
She's better than medicine, she's such a clown.
she usually takes, her troubles in stride.
This time is different, she cannot hide.
The fear she is feeling, she has been told.
To tell her family, what her future holds.
God bless you Brenda, you're in my prayers.
You've always been special, no one else compares.

CELEBRATING MOTHER'S DAY

To those who can't be with their mother,
Tomorrow on her special day.
I remember what the Pastor told us,
When our mother passed away.
He said go home, take out the family album,
Try to laugh, instead of crying.
I thought that sounds really insane,
Because inside my soul was dying.
All my brothers, and sisters, and I,
Went back to my mothers place.
We took out the family album,
I remember like it was yesterday.
We started talking and laughing hard,
About funny things, that had gone on.
It felt more like a celebration, than
the fact that our momma was gone.
If you have lost your father and mother,
Their memory will never fade away,
Just try to be happy and cheerful
Tomorrow on your mothers special day.

Changes

I was trying to write a new poem,
But my mind just drew a blank.
Maybe it's because I'm exhausted,
From packing up all these things.
I would love to rent a dumpster,
And shove all these things in.
Why do I buy all this (stuff)
It really should be a sin.
I only need my clothes, and a bed
And maybe a pot or two,
I' am trying to down size,
I don't know if one bedroom, will do.
I'll buy me a really large couch,
So my family can visit me,
It's too late to change my mind now,
I have already talked to me.

Written by my friend Ivan Stewart

CHILDHOOD DARKNESS

When darkness comes, it's time to sleep.
Then times goes by. that will not keep.
The darkness holds, the soul in right.
As it is, all through the night.
Things are lost within the mind,
And stay in check, so far behind.
Memories come, and then it's time,
To look at all things, left behind.
The darkness holds a secret, you
thought was a dream,
When darkness will turn into light,
You will start to scream.
What do I do, what do I say,
When darkness will turn back into day.
Who to turn to, I don't know.
I wish these memories, would just go.
The house so still, in the darkest hour.
When I was just a little flower.
Flowers wilt, and then decay,
When dark of night, turns into day.
At breakfast time you look around,
For the darkness to be found.
Then daylight came with sun so bright,
To take away, the darkest night.
Love this day, because when it's done,
The darkness, will replace the sun.
The darkness has a way to show,
That memories, can be hard to hold.
The memories that seem to burn,
Please be gone, do not return.
Then in the night, I always hear.
My Savior whom I love so dear.

Kentucky Memories

Memories were easy, to make in Kentucky.
Time was about all we had,
Our past is what defines us,
Whether times were happy, or sad
I can sit for hours, and reminisce,
About the things, we did for fun
Playing marbles, tag, and wading the creeks,
We stayed busy, until the day was done.
Our two-room schools, and swinging bridges,
Are becoming a thing of the past.
We have to let go of the olden days,
Our memories, can forever last.
What I wouldn't give to go back in time,
For a reunion with my loved ones,
I have to be content, with the memories,
As most of my family, are gone.
A lot of years have passed, since childhood,
I've raised a family, of my own.
Each year when I return for a visit,
It's clear the olden days, are gone.

CHRISTMAS IN THE OLD HOMEPLACE

If I could have one wish come true,
I think my wish would be,
Once more to be a child at home,
With presents, underneath the tree.
The thrill of listening for the sound,
Of Santa, and his sleigh.
The excitement and wide eyed wonder,
For the arrival of Christmas day.
The joy of having only one present,
And a bag of treats, so sweet.
Oh,to be a child once more,
Sharing Christmas,with my family.
A baby, being born in a manger,
On a cold night,so far away.
Is the reason we celebrate the season,
Let's remember this on our special day.
Oh, to be a child once again,
Sitting together, by the warm fireplace.
What a happy remembrance of family,
In the cabin, on this very special day.

Christmas Long Ago

When I was just a little child,
Simple things could make me smile.
The fireplace aglow, with hickory wood,
The crooked tree, that smelled, so good.
We didn't get a lot of toys,
Our hearts were filled with Christmas joy.
We always had a bag filled with treats,
Fruits and nuts, and candy so sweet.
Christmas sure has changed a lot,
Since I was just a little tot.
The holidays are celebrated all over the world.
For each and every boy and girl.
They still wait anxiously in their beds,
For the sounds of Santa, and his sled.
This year, may all your dreams come true,
Have a very merry Christmas,
And a happy New Year too.

CHRISTMAS TREE ANXIETY

Each year I get really excited,
To put up the Christmas tree.
But the closer,it gets to Christmas,
The tree looks different to me.
So I keep re-arranging the ornaments,
trying to make it look,just right.
Why do I put the tree up so early,
I'm so glad Christmas Eve, is tonight.
Tomorrow, after the presents, are opened,
And the guests, are headed out the door,
I'll take the boxes, from the closet,
To pack the ornaments away,once more.
Then next year on Thanksgiving,
I'll give it a little more thought,
I'll fight the urge, to put the tree up early.
I'll just hide the presents, I have bought.
So now it's the day after Christmas,
I'm so glad the children had fun.
My living room, is back in order,
And the un-decorating is done.

COLLECTING

Everyone has a collection
In one form or another
I should be the greatest cook
Because I'm a cookbook lover
I read my books from front to back
I ooh and aah at the meals
Everything looks mouth watering
Why do I cook the same things still
Beans and taters and cornbread
Biscuits and gravy is the best
Maybe I will take a book out
I'll put my skills to the test
I have my cookbooks in every room
There's boxes left unpacked
I think my collecting days are over
I may have to give some back

CRAZY THINGS WE DID

Sometimes I stop and think about,
The crazy things we did.
Growing up in Eastern Kentucky,
When we were just a kid.
Jumping on a springboard,
Flying high up in the air.
Diving in a hole of water,
Doing it on a dare.
Ignoring our mother's warning,
When she said you had better not!
Trying to play it innocent,
Just hoping she had forgot.
Swinging on a grapevine,
Hanging from a tree,
Hoping and praying it wouldn't break,
But it surely did for me.
Walking barefoot through the weeds,
Never thinking about the snakes,
We were certainly very lucky,
With all the chances we would take.
Oh, to be a child again,
And go back home and roam.
I miss all of my siblings,
We had fun,when we were small.

DAYS OF YORE

It's always fun, to go back for awhile,
And recall the things that made me smile.
The smell of meals, made fresh from scratch,
On the old coal stove, oh I'd love to go back.
To the four room cabin, that use to be,
When life was simple and so carefree.
Swinging on grapevines, wading in the creek,
Playing hop-scotch, and marbles for keeps.
When the weather turned cold, we stayed inside,
Reading, and playing, by the fireplace light.
The memory can carry us back, once more,
To the things we shared, in the days of yore.

DIXON SCHOOL

I can still remember my favorite school,
There were two rooms,each had four grades
One teacher taught first throiugh fourth,
The other teacher taught fifth thru eighth.
I remember all the teachers well,
Miss Dixon was my favorite one.
She didn't tolerate bad behavior,
We were happy when the day was done.
A memorable time of the day for me,
Was eating all the great foods.
The cook saved leftovers through the week,
And on fridays we had great soup.
We had matching outside toilets,
They were marked,his and hers.
I remember written,on the bathroom wall,
Were a lot of dirty words.
Dixon School, was a really great place.
I hold it dear,inside my heart.
If I could go back in time,
Dixon would be a great place to start

Don't Mourn My Passing

To all of those who love me,
When my life on earth is done.
Please don't mourn my passing,
All my battles,will have been won.
There will be no more depression,
No more lonliness,no more pain.
I will be in the arms of jesus,
I'll have peace and comfort again.
Remember how much I love you,
Hold me dear inside your heart.
we will all be together, again one day,
Never more will we be apart.

DREAMING

She lay contented, among the flowers,
Warmed by the morning sun.
Contemplating what her future held.
As a new day had just begun.
As she breathed the flowers sweet perfume,
She envisioned a new romance,
With a love as warm as the morning sun.
A new future, if only by chance.
She stood, and glanced, around her.
At the beauty, the earth enfolds.
What a glorious way for the day to begin,
Her future was full of hope.

DREAMS

I was dreaming last night
Of a tall handsome man
And then I awoke to reality
Oh bummer! I said to myself out loud
Why can't this be an actuality?
Dreams can be so peaceful at times
But they can also be disturbing
Sometimes I almost jump out of bed
They can be frightening and alarming
I've been told that dreams
Are what you were thinking
Before you went to sleep
I really don't agree with that at all
If it were so, life would be complete
Whatever the reason for our dreams
It would really be nice to know
Then I could have only good ones
And let the bad ones go

DREAMS

A country lane, a shady lane,
A path, this girl loved to walk.
A place to think, a place to dream.
A place to be alone.
A country girl, an innocent girl,
With thoughts beyond the hills.
A hope for love, a longing for more,
Than the mountains, could fulfil.
A girl who's dream, came true in part,
But now she dreams again.
To return to the mountains,
And walk that path, and dream
that dream again.

DUTY IN VIETNAM

He never knew the sorrow,
She kept hidden, deep inside.
When he wanted to serve his country,
And to travel, far and wide.
She never knew the anguish,
He felt as he turned to go.
With the knowledge,he may never return,
or the lump that was in his throat.
She never knew the many times,
he thought of her, as bullets flew,
Fighting in the jungles, of Viet Nam,
though it was something he wanted to do.
He never knew the many times,
She waited for mail to arrive,
Hoping for a letter to give her
proof, that he was still alive.
After several years, he made it back home,
He could now see, how she had aged.
Two tours of duty was over,
He was home now, and he was safe.

FACEBOOK CHRISTMAS

T'was a few days before Christmas,
And all over my facebook,
Were all these delicious recipes,
I knew I would have to cook.
Not a calorie was missing,
Not even any fat.
My waistline will be bigger,
I will feel like a big fat rat.
My New Year's Resolution, will be
the same as it was before.
To vow to lose all these extra pounds,
So I can fit through the front door.
So Merry Christmas, all my facebook friends,
May your waistline grow like mine.
You know I'm only kidding, your friendship is divine.
I'm just trying to spread some holiday cheer,
To everyone I have come to know,
May you have a wonderful Christmas,
And may our friends list continue
to grow.

Facebook

Facebook can sometimes,get a bad rap.
When someone posts some unwanted crap.
It can be a really good source of news,
There's recipes, bible quotes, and GOOD gossip too.
I have made a lot of special friends,
I've bored them with my poetry to no end.
There's Ivan who has a way with words,
And maybe some friends, who are a little absurd.
I still love all my facebook friends,
My new ones, and some i knew back when.
There's a site we can share our childhood years,
We talk, we laugh and shed a few tears,
Thanks to Larry johnson,for the Letcher site.
He's a modern day,Old McDonald,and he's really a riot.
I feel kind of lost, when my computer is down,
It's a friend to me, I'll keep it around.

FALL

Sitting here in my porch swing,
Listening to the birds sing.
The leaves are falling,
Jack Frost is calling,
Where did summer go?
It's a beautiful season,
But the only reason,
I want the winter to come,
Is to put up the tree, for
the grandchildren to see.
And try to enjoy, my new home.
There's no use complaining,
If it's snowing or raining.
Mother nature is the one to blame.
before you know it,
Spring will be here.
And we'll start all over again.

Fallen Heroes

They are gone, but not forgotten,
Those heroes, who died for you and me.
They sleep beneath the land they fought for,
They gave their life,to keep us free.
We can never forget our fallen heroes.
Who nobly fought,and nobly died.
Death opened the door to heaven,
They have entered the world of light.
There will always be another war,
And more brave men, will meet their fate.
It's just another part of living,
Let us remember them on Memorial Day.

FEELING LIKE I DON'T BELONG

One Sunday as I sat in church,
Looking around at everyone,
I felt I was the only one
who was feeling so alone.
I was watching couples holding hands,
As they listened to God's word.
And I thought why cant i find happiness,
before i leave this earth.
The next two Sundays I stayed at home
And lay in bed & cried.
I took my bible out & read
several chapters & then i realized
All the miracles God had performed
& all the illnesses he had healed.
I knew i had to get back to church,
There was hope for me still.
Looking back at your past in life
And regretting the mistakes you made
can make your future stronger,
because you know the price you paid.
God did a lot for all of us
we can never praise him enough.
He gave his son to die on the cross,
Let's remember that when the going is tough.

FIRST LOVE

Do you remember your first love?
The one that got away.
That special heart pounding emotion,
You think of, still today.
There can only be one first love,
If you have it, hold on tight.
The feeling can never be replaced.
No matter how hard you try.
The years pass by so quickly,
And new love will come along.
There may never be another love,
As memorable, or as strong.

FRIDAY THE THIRTEENTH

Who said, Friday the thirteenth is unlucky?
I was wondering that today.
I thought that sounded silly,
It's just another day!!
Then things started happening to me,
That made me change my mind,
I wanted to go do some shopping,
But my keys, I could not find.
Then my daughter called me from her work,
And said, Could you pick me up?
I said, Sure!, before I remembered,
I was having a little bad luck.
Finally! at last I found the keys,
Then down the road, I went,
I started hearing some, thumping,
A flat is what that meant!
Oh well, she will have to wait a bit.
On this Friday, the thirteenth.
My flat was fixed, I picked her up,
I thought we were headed home,
"Can you take me to my friends house?"
I sighed, and we headed out.
Down this road, and down that one.
I'm in trouble, there's no doubt.
At last we arrived and I asked her,
Do you think I can find my way back?

She knew, a sense of direction,
Is something I have always lacked.
"OH sure you can, is what she said,
Just make one right and a left.
Then why did she have me make all those turns?
Is what I asked myself.
So I took her advice, and I headed back home,
It didn't take long before I knew
I was in a totally different zone
Next time on Friday, the thirteenth,
If anyone asks, for a ride,
They will just have to take a taxi,
After all, I still have my pride.

FRUIT TREES

I remember well, the persimmon tree,
That stood at the top of the hill.
They were tiny, sweet and delicious.
I remember the flavor still.
My sisters and I would jump out of bed,
And race each other to the tree.
We'd find the ones, hidden in the leaves,
It was a game, for my sisters, and me.
It didn't take much to make us happy,
Candy was a sometimes treat.
With all the fruit trees in our yard,
We always had our share of sweets
Persimmon, mulberry, apples and pears,
The choice was ours, everyday.
What I wouldn't give to have them now,
But those days, have gone away.

God's Creations

If you read Genesis, you will be amazed,
By all the work God did in only six days.
He separated the darkness, and gave us light.
The light was day, the dark was night.
He put lots of stars, and planets in the sky.
The oceans he formed were deep and wide.
Oh, the power God has in his Mighty hand.
He spread vegetation, across the land.
He knew exactly what the trees would need.
To keep them producing, he gave them seeds.
He put creatures in the ocean,and animals on the land.
After all of that, for help, he created man.
From the rib of man, he created him a mate.
God was really tired, so on the seventh day.
He made it holy,and decided to rest,
We should worship on Sunday, and know we are blessed.
God will forgive us for all our sins.
Open up your heart and let him come in.
He gave his son to die on the cross,
Thank him on Sunday, because he paid the cost.
For all our sins, whether large or small.
Show God you love him, please one and all.

GOD'S WORK

In the beginning. God created Heaven, and Earth,
He separated the darkness, from the light.
When he was finished, he gave them names,
He called them, day and night.
There was water above, and water below,
Then God decided there had to be land,
When he was finished, we had land and sky,
All of this, by the power, of God's mighty hand.
He still had lot's of work to do,
So he created the plants, and the trees.
With lots of seeds to keep producing,
These things were finished, by day three.
He put creatures in the ocean, and birds in the sky,
And animals to roam the earth,
When he was finished with all the creatures,
He created, man and woman, to rule over his work.
God was exhausted, after doing all this,
He decided to rest, on the seventh day.
That's the reason, for church on Sunday,
To thank him in such a small way.

Going Back In Time

Do you ever take a walk back in time
And reminisce, about life at home.
It was a different way of living,
I'm sad to say, those days are gone.
We spent many years, in a four room cabin,
That sat far back, in the woods.
We walked three miles, to school, and back.
I would do it over, if I could.
I loved the old, coal burning stove,
It was warm, in the cold winter days.
The food momma prepared, on the old coal stove,
Seemed tastier, in so many ways.
Soup beans, cornbread, and fried potatoes,
Blackberry cobblers, and fried apple pies,
Homemade cakes, and puddings from scratch,
Fresh green beans, and ripe tomatoes on the side.
It was always drafty, in the old log cabin
When the bone chilling winds would blow.
Two fireplaces, and a wood burning stove,
Kept us warm, and protected from the cold.
In the summer we managed, to find lots to do.
Without toys, to keep us occupied.
We would wade in the creek, and swing on vines,

Play hopscotch, and make mud pies.
Growing up in Kentucky, didn't seem so bad.
Being poor was just the way of life.
Our parents worked hard, to raise us right,
They were strict, but we all survived.
We learned really fast, we didn't talk back.
Those switches, didn't feel so good.
When we were bad, we had to cut our own.
Didn't momma know, we'd cut a small one, If we could.
I know our parents, really loved us all,
Saying I love you, was something we didn't do.
It was a struggle for them, to keep us fed.
Without the words, the love shone through
Kentucky, is a place I dream about a lot,
I go back, several times a year.
It was my home, for a very long time,
The memories, I'll forever hold dear.

GOING HOME

I tell myself there's no use worrying,
About tomorrow, and what the future
may hold.
But try as I may, when I leave here tomorrow,
My heart will be heavy, and filled with sorrow.
Each time I leave, to go back home,
I have mixed emotions, I feel so alone.
I have to remember I have a family,
And friends, and church, I'm anxious to see.
We have to accept, What will be, will be.
And try to live our life, in peace.
Death is just a part of living,
Share all you can, while there's time for giving.
Good-by dear Kentucky, I will soon return,
I'll never forget the lessons, I've learned.
There's no use in grieving, over thing we have
lost,
We have to move on, no matter the cost.

GOLDILOCKS UNINVITED

When Goldilocks went over to the three bears house,
she sneaked around as quiet as a mouse.
what gave her the right to eat their food,
Didn't she know she was being rude?
The three bears were quietly minding
their own business.
That's amazing, because
Bears can be very vicious,
I often wondered how she broke baby bears chair
Does a little girl weigh more
than a baby bear?
And why was one bowl of food cold &
one hot?
I'm sure all three bowls,
were prepared in the same pot.
If Goldilocks had gotten caught
by the bears,
she could have been breakfast,
it would only be fair.
There's a lesson to be learned
from this situation,
Don't enter anyone's house,
without an invitation.

Grandchildren

Do you know a little smile you love
That lights up your whole world
We have all the love in our heart
For our grandchild, be it a boy or a girl
A little hand that pulls you along
Everywhere they want to go
Do you have someone with big innocent eyes
That seem to touch your very soul
They could melt the hardest of hearts
Whether you admit it, it is so
A pretty smile, a little hand
And eyes to ease your pain
Enjoy your grandchildren while you can
You have so much love to gain

GRANDCHILDREN

Grandchildren, are so special,
They are a gift like no other.
We can have them for a visit,
Then give them back to mother.
God knew what he was doing,
Giving children when we are young.
Because as we get older,
It's harder to keep things calm.
With all the noise they're making,
And all their bellyaching.
They're precious, and so sweet,
We love to pinch those rosy cheeks.
Yes, grandmothers were once mothers,
It's true, but it feels so great,
To keep them when we want to,
Just to give their mother a break.

GRANDMOTHER'S PASSING

God knew he had to call her home,
He knew her pain, now the pain is gone.
She's in a place, where angels sing,
He gave her peace, now she has wings.
it's lonely now, without her here.
She knows our pain, she sees our tears.
Don't cry for me, my soul's at rest.
I feel your love, your sweet caress.
Now I will spread, my wings and fly,
I'll see you on, the other side.

GROWING

Is there anything sweeter than a child?
Their innocense is so endearing.
Sometimes we want to keep them small,
to protect them from pain, and suffering.
We hold them close and try to teach them,
To know the difference from right and wrong
We have to believe we did the right thing,
And pray, we made them strong.
Life passes by so swiftly,
You turn around and you are amazed.
How did they become adults so fast?
It seems it was only days.
We always need to be thankful for,
The times we've shared with them
then when they have a child of their own,
We will be like a parent again.

Happy Father's Day

What a joyful day it would be,
To see my father, once more.
To be able to say, I love you,
When he walked through the door.
I always took my father for granted,
I didn't expect him to pass away
If your father is still with you,
Please,never forget to say,
I love you dad, and thank you,
For all you have done for me.
Show him how much he means to you,
That's all he really needs.
Father's never expect payment,
For all the things they do,
On this special day, say I love you dad,
And thank you, for just being you.

HOPE

Sometimes, on your happiest day,
When everything seems bright.
The clouds roll in and steal the sunshine,
And takes your happiness away.
Hold onto the fact, the day will pass,
Your future can be bright, once more.
You will be wrapped, in a blanket of contentment,
Where you can feel safe, and secure once more.

HOWARD VINCENT O'BRIEN

On January the eighth, nineteen, and forty two,
HOWARD VINCENT O'BRIEN, knew what he had to do.
There was a war raging, he wanted to take a stand.
When it was time to go, he took his mother's hand.
She said, HOWARD, you're still a child, you are not yet of age.
He smiled and said, Mother, the decision I've made.
Without peace mother, what good is living?
His voice was grim, but gentle, her heart was forgiving.
Where did the time go?, it seemed like only yesterday,
He had that toothless grin, and freckles on his face.
She taught him to have virtue, and the wisdom to know,
Any decision he would make, she would have to let him go.
HOWARD VINCENT O'BRIEN, died doing his part.
His Mother was proud, but it left an ache in her heart.
She said I'm proud of you Howard for taking a stand even though the years didn't show it,
You were already a man.

I WANDERED AND I WONDERED

I wandered down the hillside,
To the place I called my home.
The grass was green and freshly mowed,
On the site, where the house belonged.
I wandered up the dirt road,
To the cabin where I spent many years.
The only thing left was the chimney,
I cried a thousand tears.
I wondered where the years had gone,
When the cabin was full of life.
I'll cherish the memories, of the
homes we shared,
As family, on this mountain side.
Running and playing, and living life,
With my loved ones, who are gone.
I wondered if they were looking down,
As I climbed, back up the hill again.
This piece of land, is a special place,
I'm determined, to let go of the past.
I said good-by to that piece of land
As I wandered back to my home at last

I Can Not Sleep!

I've tossed and turned,
I wiggled and squirmed,
I counted a hundred sheep.
I still can't go to sleep!
My eyes are stuck on open,
I'm really not a joking,
Mr Sandman would you please,
Work your magic on me.
I need to be alert
I have to go to church.
Well it's five in the morning,
My clock is alarming.
My coffee is a brewing,
My biscuit i'm a chewing,
I'm slowly getting dressed,
Maybe today I will be blessed.
God, put your hand on the wheel,
And if it be your will,
I'll make it safely back,
Cause sleep is something I lack.

I MUST GO BACK

I must go back, to the old home place,
Where I spent my childhood years.
I can try to pretend, everything's the same,
My family will still be here.
I must go back to see my father,
Walking home from working in the mine.
With some penny candy, in his lunch pail,
Covered with dust, but tasted so fine.
I must go back to see my mother,
As she rocked her babies to sleep.
And to see her cooking all hours of the day,
Making sure we had plenty to eat.
I must go back, just one more time,
If only through the windows of my mind,
I could tell my momma, about all my heartaches,
She would tell me, everything will be fine.
I wish I could go back, and tell my parents,
Thank you for all you did for me,
I hope you knew, how much I loved you,
I didn't say it, but I hope you knew.

I Remember When

Remember when the roosters crowed?
And there never seemed to be grass to mow?
The yard always seemed really neat.
It was bare from ten sets of feet.
My mother swept it with a broom,
It was as neat as our bedroom.
We would walk to school, and back again.
Life sure was simple, way back when.
Our dresses were made from pretty feed sacks,
Mama saved them all summer, and put them back,
When she saved enough for our school clothes,
Off to the neighbours house we would go.
Our neighbour sewed our clothes for free,
She was very kind and neighbourly.
I like to sit and think of,Back then.
I miss those days, I wish they were here
Again

IF TIME COULD STAND STILL

If it were possible, for time to stand still,
There would be no more family, buried on the hill.
Life is not a fairytale; we have to accept it's all God's will.
He gave his only begotten son, in order that we may live,
There is no power here on earth, that's greater than God's love.
So live each and every day, and work at earning his trust.
Sometimes it's hard to live our lives,
Without whining and complaining,
We have to try to remember, that God is always reigning.
I'll say good-by to my family, once more,
And live my life to the fullest,
Until I see my family, once more,
I'll thank God, for the ways I am blessed.

INSOMNIA

It's 3 A.M. and I am listening,
To the pitter patter, of the rain.
I think the old insomnia bug,
Has bitten me again.
Why is it so impossible,
To get eight hours of sleep?
The stress, is putting wrinkles on me,
I'm so tired of counting sheep.
So I thought I would jot it down,
And maybe when I am done,
I'll try my best to relax a bit,
Then sleep will surely come.
Now it's four A.M., and here I lay,
With pen and paper in hand.
Trying to pass an hour or two,
But sleep is eluding me again.
I may as well accept the fact,
And crawl out of my bed.
I'll make some coffee to perk me up,
I'll make plans for the day ahead.

It's Never Too Late

As I sit in silence, and ponder,
my life, as it has come to be.
I ask myself if I have given, all
that was expected of me.
Could I be a better person?
if I could begin anew,
Would I try to live my life different?
Is there any more I could do?
Love is all I have to give,
There's no price for giving your heart.
Show all your love, while you still can,
It's never too late to start.

KENTUCKY PROUD

I was raised in Kentucky.
Way back in the sticks
I'm proud to say,
I'm a country hick.
In a four room cabin,
with coal for heat
We hugged the fireplace,
To warm our feet
When the fires died, we
snuggled in the bed.
The cabin was drafty, and
our noses turned red.
Waiting for papa to get out of bed,
Momma in the kitchen,
Preparing our meals.
On the old coal stove,
I can taste it still.
Homemade biscuits, and
fried smoke bacon.
Fresh eggs from the henhouse,
And a skillet full of gravy.
Then it was off to school,
Through the rain or snow.
Down the hill,
and up the track we'd go.
The two room school,

was a special place
The memories of those years
will never be erased.
The friends I made were only a few.
We grew up together,
in that two room school.
Coal mining was the only way to survive.
After years of work,
the dust took my father's life.
Most of my family have passed away.
The life we shared will be with me always.
Yes, life in Kentucky was a hard way of living,
I will never forget, the memories I've been given.

LET IT SNOW

Oh the weather outside is frightful,
The snow isn't really delightful,
I don't really have any place to go,
So let it snow, let it snow, let it snow!
I hope the children have fun outside,
When they take their sled for a ride,
I really prefer to stay inside,
So,let it snow, let it snow, let it snow!
I wish it could be spring or fall,
I don't like it hot or cold at all.
So if you like it ten below,
Let it snow, let it snow, let it snow!
I will stay inside and read a book,
I'll open the curtains, just to take a look.
If you don't really mind the cold,
Let it snow, let it snow, let it snow!!!

LET US GO BACK

Let us go back to the memories,
that are pocketed, in our mind.
The joys we collected, in our childhood,
Never fading with the passing of time.
Let us return to the Christmas,
That remains the best of times,
The excitement and thrill of waiting,
For that special gift, that would be all mine.
Poverty didn't dim, the happiness,
One unwrapped present could bring,
A brown paper bag, filled with candy
To a child, was the favourite thing.
Let us go back, to the visions,
of the fireplace, and glow of the tree,
With all of the family together,
Enjoying dinner, on Christmas Eve.
Let us return to the real meaning,
that has gotten lost, along the way.
The birth of the baby called Jesus,
In a cold stable, on this special day.

Life As A Child

Swinging on a grapevine,
Playing hide and seek,
Tying strings on a june bug,
Wading in the creek
Just a few of the many things,
we did to have some fun.
Feeling really contented,
When the day was finally done.
Catching lots of fireflies,
Putting them in a jar,
Lying on the bed at night,
Watching shooting stars.
Life was a lot of fun
When I was just a child.
It's nice to go back again.
If only for a while.
Eating all the nuts and fruits,
Growing wild in the woods,
it'd be fun to be a child again,
I would do it again, if I could.

LITTLE SNOWFLAKES

Little snowflakes, falling from the sky,
Painting the ground in white.
Each one of you, with your own design,
Reflecting in the sunlight.
Little children, excited to see,
The beauty, you create on the land.
Giving joy to all of God's angels,
With the wonder of his mighty hand.
Little raindrops, falling to the ground,
A sign, that spring is nigh.
Washing away the beauty, of the snow,
Making way for the flowers to arrive.
Little robins, singing in the trees,
What a beautiful sound to hear,
Everything is green, and blooming,
Proof, that spring is near.

LOSING WEIGHT

I NEED TO LOSE A FEW POUNDS,
I TOLD MYSELF TODAY.
MY CLOTHES ARE GETTING TIGHTER,
I DON'T KNOW HOW MUCH I WEIGH.
I CAN'T AFFORD A NEW WARDROBE,
EXERCISE HAS TO BE MY GOAL.
MAYBE I'LL START BY WALKING,
BUT THE WEATHER IS GETTING COLD.
THE HARDEST THING ABOUT WALKING,
IS WHEN YOU GET BACK HOME,
YOU HEAD STRAIGHT TO THE PANTRY,
THEN UNDO, THE WORK YOU'VE DONE.
MAYBE I'LL BECOME A VEGETARIAN,
I DON'T HAVE TO EAT RED MEAT.
AND I CAN GO ONE STEP FURTHER,
I'LL GIVE UP ALL MY SWEETS.
I'LL HAVE TO PONDER THAT FOR AWHILE,
THAT'S THE HARDEST DECISION I'VE MADE,
EVEN THOUGH I AM A DIABETIC,
I WOULD HAVE TO GIVE UP ALL MY CAKES.
THICK OR THIN, LARGE OR SMALL,
BEAUTY, MAY BE ONLY SKIN DEEP,
WE JUST HAVE TO REMEMBER,
IT'S GOOD HEALTH WE NEED TO KEEP.

LOUIS (LOU_EE)

Tori has a new little puppy,
He's as cute as he can be.
I ask her what his name was,
She said his name was Louis.
The last little puppy, that Tori named,
was probably as confused as me.
She said I'm going to call him Kitty!
I thought, are you kidding me?
Here Kitty, Kitty, come and get your food,
Is the way she called him to eat,
In a flash she had a dozen cats,
Standing at her feet.
Why didn't she give him a common name,
Like Rover, Spike, or Spot.
I hope little Louis likes his name,
He's stuck with it, like it or not.

LUCK

Find a penny, pick it up,
All day long you'll have good luck.
Oh how I wish, that was really true.
Our misfortunes, would be very few.
You can find pennies, everywhere you look,
How great, if that was all it took.
The four leaf clovers are hard to find,
And the rabbit's foot!!,oh never mind.
Of course there's the bad luck.
We have to be really wary,
If a black cat crosses your path,
It can be really scary.
If you break a mirror, seven years of bad luck.
You can't walk under a ladder!
Who makes all this stuff up?!!
There's really no such thing,
as good luck or bad. Just watch your
step, there's opportunities to be had.

MEMORIES

Our memory, can be a special place,
Where we can recall our yesterdays
The things we shared, the good, and the bad,
We can re-live it, in quiet ways.
In the dark of night, we can dream once more,
Of the mountains, majestic, and tall.
The sound of the water, as it rolled down the creek,
We can choose, what we want to recall.
It is best to dream, of the happy times,
Like the faces, of those we can see no more.
The smells, and warmth, of our Kentucky home.
We can leave the bad, in the days of yore.
Our memories are forever, a part of our past.
It's nice, every once in awhile.
To go back to the times, when life was simple,
To remember things, with a laugh, and a smile.

MINE AND EMMA'S POEM

There was a little girl,
She had a little curl,
That is all the hair she had,
She felt really, really sad.
She took some super glue,
And the strings out of her shoe.
She glued them to her head,
Then she lay down, on her bed.
When she awoke the next day,
On the pillow where she lay,
Were the strings out of her shoes,
And her only curl too.
She decided to stay bald,
Because bald is beautiful after all.

MISSING BRENDA

Sometimes life can be so tough,
When the ones you love pass on
I lost my best friend Brenda,
When God decided to call her home.
It makes no difference, the faith you have,
Or the knowledge we all must die.
It's hard to fill, the void it leaves,
When you've said your last goodbye.
Brenda was the one I always leaned on,
When I was feeling down, and so alone.
Her sunny attitude, made me smile,
When everything was going wrong.
I miss my goofy sister Brenda,
her memory will never fade.
God take care of Brenda and tell her.
I'll see her again someday.

MOVING DAY

Moving is such a monotonous job,
It's hard for me to imagine,
Where I got all this junk,
From knick knacks to door knobs.
I have been collecting for many years,
From here, and there, and yonder,
Did I really want all these things,
Sometimes I have to wonder.
They look so pretty sitting there,
I can't turn and walk away.
I'll donate them to a charity,
When I move to my new place,
I've packed a zillion boxes,
And there's at least a dozen more.
I know I'm going to miss them,
Maybe I'll keep just three or four.

MY NEW HOME

The time is getting closer, for
me to leave my homeplace.
I'm not quiet sure how i am feeling,
But I must pick up the pace.
I have to live for me now,
My children are all grown.
They hope that I will keep it,
Even though their father is gone.
I will always hold fond memories,
I think it's time for me to move on.
i've lived here for twenty seven years,
The answer could be in a new home.
I need to find some solitude,
Maybe a place that's peaceful, and quiet.
It takes more than a house and land
to feel everything is going to be alright
I will pray for God to show me the answer.
As I face my new life alone.
With him in my corner, I can make the right choice,
I don't think he will let me go wrong.

MY BROTHER SAM (BO)

My brother Bo,was very excited,
To reach his seventeenth birthday.
He wanted to join the army,
To serve his country,in some way.
Our country was fighting a battle,
He wanted to take a stand,
To defend our freedom the best he could,
He wanted to travel,to foreign lands.
The day he left,my momma cried,
He was her eldest son,
She knew she wouldn't see him again,
Until the battle was won.
His first tour of duty was in Korea,
Where he married a beautiful girl,
When he excitedly left for Viet Nam,
He felt like the luckiest man in the world.
Things don't always stay the same,
They can change,in just a day,
His tour soon ended,he went back to Korea,
He had missed his son's birth-date.
Things went great for awhile,
but he wanted to go back,

To Viet Nam, for another tour,
Serving his country was his first choice,
Leaving his family, was hard to endure.
He served, then made it back to Korea,
His family he could not find,
Why? or Where, no one would know,
He had to leave his wife, and child behind.
he came home to Kentucky, and never returned,
He started drinking, to ease the pain,
He became a recluse, in the old cabin,
His happiness, he never regained again.
His only dream was to serve his country,
He had scars, though he never complained.
Somewhere in Korea, I hope his son knows,
That his father is free from pain.

MY FIRST LOVE

I never knew love until I met you.
You opened my heart, with all that you do.
Your kindness, your caring,
Your smile melts my heart. It hurts
deep inside, because we're apart.
I will love you forever, even though we can't be.
I will remember you always, please
don't ever forget me.

FATE

If I could have, one wish come true,
I would spend my life, just loving you.
Fate brought us together, fate will keep us apart.
Nothing can keep me from giving you my heart.
I'll cherish your kisses, for as long as I live.
You gave me fond memories,
There's nothing more you can give.

GRANDDAUGHTER VICTORIA

Victoria, is such a beautiful girl,
She's wise beyond her years.
At times she can be very vocal,
About the things, she sees and hears.
She hasn't had a normal life,
Yet she has a very level head.
She's talented, and inspiring,
Oh, the books that she has read.
I hope all of her dreams come true,
I love her with all my heart,
She can have a wonderful future,
She already has a great start.
Dreams can come true,in your life,
if you try hard to succeed.
And trying hard, Victoria has,
For the life she wishes to lead,
there's lots of people who love her,
I'm sure she already knows,
I want to be around a very long time,'
So I can see her future grow.

MY CHILDHOOD CABIN

Nestled between two mountain peaks,
Where the trees grow, tall and straight.
Stood a rustic, four room cabin,
Where I spent my childhood days.
Now and then my mind wanders back
To those memorable days once again.
I visit for awhile, and try to remember,
How we managed to survive, back then.
I can share with you, my treasured memories.
Though it's hard to know where to start.
Growing up in the hollows of Kentucky.
Holds a special placeman my heart.
Time spent playing in the creeks, with my siblings,
And creating our kind of fun.
Is worth more to me than all the wealth.
When everything is said and done.
I have said, good-by to so many loved ones,
As the years have passed swiftly by.
I still hold my memories, close to my heart.
Until I have said my last good-by

MY NIECE JENNY

Sometimes it's easy to forget, how fast,
Our life can be taken away.
We've got to show our loved ones,
How much we love them everyday.
I got a call this afternoon,
that took me by surprise,
My beautiful, great niece jenny,
Had suddenly lost her life.
She was my sister's pride and joy,
A very beautiful girl.
I know she's with her grandmother now.
They have left this troubled world.
Lord, please watch over Jenny,
And make sure she will be okay
Hold her mother in your arms tonight,
And take all her heartaches, away

My Old Kentucky Home

On the cold winter days,
In my old Kentucky Home
The fireplace felt so good.
When your back was warm,
your front was cold,
We would stand all day,
if we could.
We would sit all day,
And roast sweet potatoes,
In the ashes, underneath the grate.
With homemade butter, from
the neighbours farm,
The taste was worth, the long wait.
We would trudge outside, to
the cold outhouse,
And shiver, and shake all the way.
When you are, born and raised
in the mountains of Kentucky,
To us, it was just another day.
When the fires died down,
The cabin was really cold,
Our noses, would turn bright red.
We huddled together, and told ghost stories,
We stayed warm, with the quilts, on the bed.
When we awoke in the morning,
there was ice in the bucket,
Of drinking water, brought in from the spring.
The memories I'll cherish as long as I live,
because we can never, go back again.

MY OLD KENTUCKY HOMES

My old Kentucky homes are gone,
But it still feels like home to me.
I'm going back, just one last time,
For a visit, with my family.
The houses have fallen, it's not the same,
As it was many years ago.
My mind tells me, stay where your loved ones are.
They have all my heart, and soul,
I would love to go back, just one last time.
To sit at the table, once again.
With my mom and dad, and brothers, and sisters,
The way it was, way back then.
The memories I have, as a child in Kentucky,
Are etched forever in my mind.
The good times, the bad times,
I can recall them all,
They will remain with the passing of time.

My Talk With Brenda

Hello Brenda, what's Heaven like?
No one knows,until they are there.
I hope you're enjoying the tree of life,
I'm sure there's Angels everywhere,
Now that you are in Heaven,
You can walk those streets of gold.
Your eyes have 20/20 vision,
Your body has been made whole.
It's sad down here without you,
I can't call you on the phone.
mom and Dad and all our loved ones,
Will keep you from being alone.
I miss you more than words can say,
You were my very best friend.
I'll keep you dear, inside my heart,
Enjoy Heaven, until I see you again.

MY TWO ROOM SCHOOL

Down the hill, and up the tracks,
We would stay seven hours and then walk back.
Down the track, and up the hill,
I wish that I could do it still.
It mattered not, if it rained or snowed.
To the two room school,we had to go.
I made great friends, but only afew.
Everyone walked to the two room school.
There were memories made, that are here to stay,
I can see my classroom, still today.
We had two outhouses, his, and hers.
on the wall, was written dirty words.
My favorite teacher, was stern, but nice.
If you misbehaved, she didn't warn you twice.
It made her mad, if you saw and tattled,
The guilty one, and you got the paddle.
With no air conditioning to keep us cool,
I still loved my little two room school.
The mountains and railroad track remain.
But my favorite school is not the same.
It's still standing, though it's become a home.
The looks have changed, but the memories remain.
I know that I can never go back,
To my two room school, near the railroad tracks.

NATURE

Nature can be a beautiful thing,
We love the colors, each season brings.
In the spring all of the buds pop out,
It is a beautiful time, there is no doubt.
There's so much beauty, everywhere,
The scent from the flowers fill the air.
Of all the flowers, I love the rose.
Their many different colors, are a sight to behold.
Summer has lots of beauty too,
When the trees are green, and the skies are blue.
All the birds are singing, in the trees.
The robins, the sparrows, the chick-a-dees.
Autumn is the most beautiful time of all,
The leaves change colors and begin to fall.
Winter is beautiful, even though it's cold.
The crispness in the air and the falling snow.
Mother nature is a special gift to us.
It was all created, by God, up above.

NIGHT TIME

At night time, when the sky is bright,
With all of God's illumined light.
I say a prayer, I dream a dream,
About things that were, and what could have been.
Time can ease the hurt, and pain.
Then inner peace, you can regain.
Life is short, we must not waste,
Our time remaining, it passes in haste.
Our fate is in God's mighty hands,
We may not see, or yet understand.
The dawn will break, to a brighter day,
And take the night time, dreams away.

NOSTALGIC TIMES

I think at times, I can still hear,
My father stoking the fires at night.
The noise of the poker, shifting the embers,
To give air,for the new coal to light.
The sound of our mother whipping up breakfast,
While we snuggled under the quilts,
Waiting for the heat from the coal stove,
In the kitchen, to take away the chill.
The smell of biscuits, baking in the oven,
Smoked bacon frying in the pan,
Seemed to be much more inviting,
Why? I just can't understand.
The rustic log cabin, with the noisy tin roof,
And wind whistling through the cracks,
Still seems much better than the modern day homes,
For a while, I would love to go back.

Written by Ivan Stewart

One Cold Night In December

A December night. and mighty cold,
A stranger came to call.
Ragged and tagged in coveralls,
That looked about to fall.
A weathered old man, with a shaggy beard,
Had asked for a bite to eat,
A look at his face so cold and red,
And shoes that looked deplete.
Please come in sir and sit down here,
And try to warm your feet.
I asked him where he came from,
Which he said, I don't recall,
Just here and there and everywhere,
To look at one and all.
He sat to soup and sandwich, that
I prepared for him.
With every bite, to my delight,
I thought of angel hymns.
I ask to take his coat off,
There was then a small reply,

Thank you sir, you are so kind,
But now I must say good-by
My travels have just started,
There's so much more to see.
People, places, kindness,
and all that's come to be.
I walked him to the door,
and saw him out of sight.
Those angel hymns, that I first heard,
were coming in the night.
The night became a glowing, and
I looked up to the stars.
One that was a showing,
much brighter and by far.
Did an angel come to visit or
Was it just in my mind?
When angels come to visit, what
do they hope to find?

ORCHARD BRANCH, KENTUCKY

One of my favorite places to live,
When I was growing up,
Was a place called Orchard Branch, in Kentucky,
A place you couldn't help but love.
we had a huge apple orchard.
We couldn't wait for the fruit to get ripe.
There were red ones, green ones, sweet and sour,
We all had a different one, we liked.
When momma said we couldn't go,
Into the orchard, all alone,
Temptation can be a really bad thing,
Though we knew what would be waiting at home.
We knew we would all get a switching,
We begged but it did no good,
When we disobeyed,there was no bargaining,
I knew we would do it again when we could.
When momma said, don't wade in the creek,
The temptation was hard to resist,

It was fun for awhile, but we knew what was waiting,
She would meet us with a painful switch.
I know it sounds like times were bad,
But our momma was just concerned,
She was trying to keep us safe and secure,
It was a lesson we all had to learn.
If I could have my dream come true,
I'd go back to Orchard Branch,
I would do my best, to obey my mother,
I would give her all my thanks.

PEACE

If all the countries, could just get along,
In this crazy, mixed up world.
There would be no more killing,
No more pain and suffering,
For the innocent little boys and girls.
They didn't choose to be born,
In a world full of turmoil,
Where war and destruction reigns,
My hope is that one day, peace will be found,
And the deaths were not in vain.
May God bless, all the angels
That are with him now,
He knows they're in a better place.
We don't understand, the reason things happen,
we just know, it's all by God's grace.

POETRY

I have often wondered, how
poets write, such amazing poetry.
I have learned, the way I'm feeling,
Determines the outcome for me.
if you should read all of my attempts,
At writing all my thoughts down
You would find there's lots of sad ones
Happy ones may not be found.
I wish there was a magic wand,
To change my mood when I'm writing,
I prefer to write amusing ones,
I find they're much more exciting.
My favorite books to read to my children,
When they were very small,
Were the ones that was written by Dr. Seuss,
He's the most amusing poet of all.
it's three A.M.,in the morning,
As I'm writing this poem for you,
My caffeine is doing it's job now,
I'm feeling a little less blue.
I enjoy sharing my poems, with you,
But I hope you will understand,
If they are happy, or depressing, long, or short,
As I take pen and paper, in hand.

PRAYING

Have you ever tried to say a prayer,
But the words just wouldn't come.
You wanted to ask God for forgiveness,
For the wrong things you have done.
Praying should come from deep inside,
We can't rehearse the words to say.
Don't wait until there's a reason,
We should do it everyday.
God can understand our prayers,
Even if we search for the words.
He knows, already, the things we have done,
Our words will always be heard.
If you are looking for forgiveness,
Open your mind, and let it flow,
Don't worry about what you say,
As long as it comes from your soul.

Restless Soul

There are times i have to wonder,
Where do I call home,
Is it in my Kentucky birthplace,
Or anywhere I choose to roam.
My soul is always restless,
I go back, every now and then,
To my old home in the mountains,
I can reminisce, and remember when.
I try to feel at ease there,
Though time has helped me to see,
That home is not the same now,
It's not the place, where I need to be.
My children, are in north Carolina,
I've been here for twenty seven years.
I have to stay where my heart is,
Though i have shed a lot of tears.
A restless soul can't be happy,
As much as I want to be,
Maybe one day, I'll find the answer,
For the turmoil, inside of me.
Where has all the years gone?
it seems like yesterday,
I was a happy child in Kentucky,
Those days seems to have faded away.

SOOTHING DREAMS

It seems to me, I sometimes hear,
A warm voice whispering, come to me dear.
I can take you away, to a better place.
where your fears and worries, can be replaced.
With a love as strong as the raging sea.
Then your dreams, can become a reality.
There will be no pain, where I'm taking you.
Come with me now, your life will be renewed.
I awake from a tranquil moment, and find.
it was a soothing dream, I must leave in my mind.

SPANKINGS

Spankings were a daily occurrence,
When I was a child at home.
Was it for general purposes,
Or did we always do something wrong.
I thought I was a really good kid
I tried to never talk back.
Momma seemed to love our squirming,
When the switches were striking our legs.
Our legs seemed to look like a zebra,
There was no use for us to beg.
Being a mother was wasn't easy back then,
With no modern day conveniences to use.
She worked really hard to keep us safe,
I admired my mother,it was a hard
time to get through

SPECIAL LOVE

Do you remember, your first love?
The one that slipped away.
That special heart pounding emotion,
You think of, still today.
There can only be one first love,
If you have it, hold on tight.
That love can never be replaced,
No matter how hard you try.
The years will pass so quickly,
New loves will come along,
There will never be another love,
As memorable, or as strong.

Swinging Bridges And Dreams

Standing on a swinging bridge
After a storm rolls by.
With the water raging, fast and furious,
gave the illusion, that i could fly.
the bridge seemed to be moving upstream,
I would spread my arms, and pretend,
I was sailing away, to a better place,
Where a new life I could begin.
The swinging bridges are disappearing,
With the passing of time, it seems.
We can't hold back the changing,
We can still, hold onto our dreams.

TEAR DROPS AND HEARTACHES

If teardrops were pennies,
I could have a lot of wealth.
if Heartaches were stories,
I would have a lot to tell.
if I could take all my past,
And put it on a slate,
I could wipe away all the heartaches,
and start over, with no mistakes.
But that is just a fairytale life,
Bad choices can't be erased.
The tear drops are a comfort,
To ease the pain of the heartaches.

THANK YOU GOD!

Thank you God, for the gift you gave,
Thank you God, for lost lives you save.
When troubled times,make my faith grow weak,
Thank you God for your love I seek.
When war time brings so much death and pain,
I always remember, God, you are not to blame.
You gave us life, you don't make our choices
When we need you God, I know you hear our voices.
So, thank you God, for the air I breathe,
For the stars that shine, and the beautiful trees.
Without you God, where would I be?
You gave your only, son for me.
Thank you god, for your warm embrace,
Your unconditional love, and your Amazing Grace.

THANK YOU MOMMA & DADDY

Momma, did I say I love you,
For all the many years
you managed to keep us fed & contented,
I'm sure you had a lot of fears.
Did I tell you that I was so thankful?
for the hands that look so worn,
and the many times I saw you crying,
I know you felt forlorn,
If I didn't tell you that I love you,
Momma I hope you understand
It is only because I didn't hear it,
forgive me momma if you can.
Daddy did I say I love you
For the many scars that showed.
From working in the coal mines
In the darkness, danger & cold.
Daddy just remember this.
Even when things were so wrong
you tried your best to protect us,
you tried your best to make us strong.
Momma & daddy thank you again,
For the life you gave to me
Even if we never said I love you,
it was there for me to see.

THANKSGIVING DINNER

Thanksgiving dinner,oh what a treat
There's turkey and lots of trimmings to eat.
I think this year, I will take a break,
I'll let someone else cook, for goodness sake!!
Why does it have to be mama's place,
To slave over the stove so they can stuff their face.
Not to mention, all the dirty plates.
Do they help wash them?,oh no way.
It takes all day to cook the food.
They eat, then off to the couch, their glued!
When mama's in the kitchen, slaving away,
They're sitting and waiting, for pies and cakes.
Togetherness, is a wonderful thing,
It's my turn to be treated like a queen,
So next Thanksgiving, when they look for me.
They just may find me at Mickey,D's
I do not like turkey, and pumpkin pies,
I'd rather have a burger, and a order of fries.
In case my children, are reading this ditty,
Don't worry, I'm only trying to be witty.
Just bring a dish, to help me out,
After all, sharing, is what it's all about.

THAT SPECIAL FRIEND

It's nice to turn back the clock,
for just a little while,
To remember that special someone,
Who always made you smile.
A friend you could confide in,
to share your hopes and dreams.
Those friends can never be replaced,
They are few, and far between.
years may come, and years may go,
New friends will come along.
But there will always be the memory of,
That friend who is forever gone.
Our heart can be filled with fondness,
As we look back, and review,
The special moments, you cherish,
With the special friend, you knew.

THE BEAUTIFUL SEASONS

There is a beauty in the seasons,
Each in their own way.
Everyone has a favorite,
Though I can truthfully say,
Autumn is the one I love the most,
The trees are a sight to behold.
The leaves turn, many different colors,
Red, yellow, orange, and gold.
It's cool in the morning and,
And warm in the afternoon,
It's a really good indication,
Cold weather is coming soon.
Winter is a really beautiful season,
Even though it feels very cold,
Each and every child in the nation,
Is waiting impatiently, for the snow.
They know it's almost christmas,
When snowflakes begin to fall.
There's excitement like no other,
When Santa Claus, comes to call.
Spring is a wonderful season,
There's always a cool,cool breeze,
All the flowers, and trees are blooming,
There's blossoms, on the trees,
Before long, it's summer again,
It's just too hot for me,
Everyone goes on vacation,
to the mountains or to the beach.
Soon we are back where started,
we are dreaming of the fall,
It's still my very favorite season,
I love Autumn most of all.

THE BEAUTY OF KENTUCKY

In the Kentucky mountains,
It's a beautiful scene,
Before all the trees,
have turned to green.
You can see for miles, and miles away,
Walking the trails, on a clear sunny day.
Kentucky has many wonders to behold,
The mountain peaks, and the valleys below.
I can sit for hours, and admire the view.
In the early morning,
When the fog rolls through.
Then springtime comes with a beauty unseen,
The flowers are blooming,
The trees are turning green.
Springtime, summer, winter or fall,
There's a beauty in the seasons,
I love them all.

THE BLUE GRASS STATE

Kentucky is the Blue grass state,
Where the mountains are so tall,
It makes the sun rise late.
Where everyone talks with a southern drawl,
Like howdy folks, and come back y'all
Where the shucky beans, are oh so sweet.
The southern hospitality, just can't be beat.
Where the country churches, are small but proud,
Any more than a few, makes a crowd.
Where the swinging bridges, are hard to find,
And work is dwindling, in the Kentucky coal mine.
Things are changing; it's plain to see,
But it will always be home to me.

THE COAL MINER'S LIFE

The life of a coal miner,
Is the hardest life I know.
There's a danger like no other,
Crawling around in that dark hole.
The miner doesn't think about,
His future and what it holds,
His only thought is making a living,
To keep his family clothed.
He doesn't worry about the caveins,
Or the coal dust on his lungs,
He's just proud that he is working,
For his wife, and daughters and sons.
My father was a coal miner,
I remember his job very well.
Sometimes when he came home from work
He would open his dinner pail,
Inside would be some penny candy,
What a treat it was for us kids,
I'm proud to be a coal miner's daughter,
And all the hard work,he did.

THE DANDELION

The dandelion is a beautiful sight
When the wind blows sheets of gold
And the memory of my first bouquet
That my childrens hand did hold
I'll forever cherish my childrens eyes
Their excitement as they ran to me
With broken little yellow dandelions
Placed in my hand so carefully
Those wild flowers were worth more than gold
Or all the roses money could buy
I took my dandelions and cherished them
If your a mother you can understand why

THE DEEP DARK HOLE

Down into the darkness,
The coal miner goes.
Wading through the water,
In that deep dark hole
Down on his knees he goes,
When the top is way too low,
Trying to make a living,
Working in that hole.
It's a dangerous job
Every miner knows.
His life is on the line,
As he enters that hole.
With God by his side,
And family on his mind.
He will make it back out,
When the day is done.
To see loved ones again,
In the warm and bright sun.
God bless the coal miner,
The years take a toll,
With the dust in his lungs,
From the deep dark hole.

THE KENTUCKY MINE

Stop for a moment, and try to imagine,
What life was like years ago.
If our fathers had not made a living,
Working in the Kentucky coal.
I am thankful, for the coal mines,
It was the only way to survive.
The coal kept us fed, and warm at night,
though many coal miners, lost their lives.
times are changing, now it seems,
The coal mines, are shutting down.
I can only imagine, what Kentucky will be,
when there's no more jobs around.
I don't pretend to understand, the why's
and wherefores of it all
God bless the coal miner, everywhere,
it's sad to see you take the fall.

THE LITTLE GIRL (IN A TATTERED DRESS)

A little girl, in a tattered dress,
And shoes, sewn with white thread.
Felt really pretty, when she left for school,
Until she heard what her teacher said.
I have a gift to give to you,
I want to help you if I can
The little girl, looked so confused,
She didn't quite understand.
The teacher gave the little girl,
A box, that smelled so sweet,
She carried that box,all the way home,
She couldn't wait to take a peek.
Inside was something so beautiful,
She gasped, for she was so surprised.
There were sweaters that smelled like lavender,
And a pretty dress, that made her cry.
She couldn't wait for the new morning to arrive
Her eyes were overflowing with tears,
She would never forget this special day.
It would stay with her for many years,
She wore those sweaters, and cherished them,
The fondness for her teacher remained
I'm that little girl in the tattered dress
My love for her is still fresh today.

THE LONESOME CHIMNEY

For more than a hundred years,
Through storms, and bitter cold.
This chimney never wavered,
To warm us, body and soul.
It stands all alone today,
With no walls for company.
All covered with vines and bushes,
What a lonesome sight to see.
If this chimney could tell a story,
What secrets it could unfold,
It's only a reminder of years gone by,
Standing there, so strong and bold.
Sitting by the firelight,
I dreamed of my future life.
Lost in the flickering embers,
For hours, as time passed by.
It's more than stone and mortar,
It's a part of my childhood years,
goodbye dear chimney, I love you.
I say, through many tears.

THE MOUNTAINS

Way down in the valley,
between two mountain peaks.
You can hear the roaring waters,
Of the overflowing creeks.
On a hot and humid, summer day,
After the storms, pass by,
The steam from the water hovers,
Between the tree tops, and
the blue summer sky.
The mountains hold many wonders,
Each season that rolls around,
In the springtime, when the
trees are in blossom,
In the fall, when leaves
are red, yellow,and brown.
In the winter when the trees are bare,
You can see tree tops for miles away.
There's always beauty in the mountains,
I'm going back to visit, one day.

THE NEW YEAR

May the new year be much brighter,
May your hopes and dreams come true,
May we keep those resolutions,
To live better the whole year through.
May we spread a little sunshine,
To all of those in pain.
May we vow to be a better person,
There's so much joy to gain.
May we show our appreciation,
To the one who gave us life.
The new year can be much better,
If our resolution is to live it right.

THE OLD DAYS

Sometimes, it's fun to think about,
My life as it was years ago.
We didn't have, a lot of things,
But what we had, was worth, more than gold.
I loved the old cast iron stove.
What I wouldn't give today,
to have one, in my kitchen.
I treasure them, in so many ways.
It was really uncomfortable, in the summertime,
We always complained, about the heat.
During the winter, in the cold log cabin,
The heat was a welcome treat.
Our cook stove, always sat cornerwise,
And on many, a cold day,
I would crawl behind the stove to read.
My favorite book, or just to play,
all the things, we had, back when,
Are really, nostalgic today,
The modern day inventions make life easier,
And replaced the old ones along the way.

The Outhouse

I'm sure there's lots of Kentuckians,
Who remember the old outhouse.
Each one has it's own history.
If you know what I'm talking about.
The outhouse sat, far away from the house,
For reasons, I'm sure you know.
We had to keep, the odors away
when the winds began to blow.
There were no lights, inside to see,
That worked out well, during the day.
But at night, when you felt the urge to go,
You just prayed, it would go away.
There's only so much a bladder can hold,
so out we would go in the dark.
The moon seemed to cast eerie shadows,
You could count the beats, of your heart.
Then there's a reason, for the catalog
toilet paper, was something we lacked.
We couldn't afford to place any orders,
It was softer than the brown paper sack.
The best thing about the outhouse,
was the fact that it was reusable
we would dig a hole in another spot.
And move it when the other was full.
outhouses are certainly rare these days,
They;ve become a thing of the past.
Thank the good lord,for indoor plumbing,
but the memory of the outhouse will last.

THE PORCH SWING

Sitting on the front porch swing,
After the night has arrived.
listening to the whipperwill,
Watching the stars in the sky.
It's a peaceful kind of feeling,
Just you, and the sounds of the night.
the creaking of the porch swing,
seems a little eerie, in the moonlight.
I loved the old front porch swing,
When the children were sound asleep.
Just another fond remembrance,
of the past, I will always keep.
There's something special, about the porch swing,
When you're sitting alone in the dark.
Dreaming of what your future holds,
And wishing upon a star.

THE ROCKING CHAIR

The squeaking of the rocking chair,
Sometimes went on all night.
As the mother rocked her crying baby,
Clasped to her breast so tight.
She sang them soothing lullabies,
As she rocked her baby, to sleep.
The hours dragged on so slowly,
Until the light through the window, peeked.
The love a mother has for her children,
Never changes, as the years pass by.
she will soothe their hurts, and heartaches,
And hold them when they cry.
Remember her in her golden years,
For the love your mother, gave to you.
The day will come, when you can rock your mom,
And sing her a lullaby too.

THE SEA OF DESPAIR

Have you ever felt, like you are lost,
In a sea of broken dreams.
There's no course for you to follow,
No hope up ahead, it seems.
You struggle for a way out,
Of the swirling waves of despair,
you're drowning in a sea of heartaches,
With no escape, anywhere.
The only hope for a future,
is to put your faith, in God's hands.
The waves of despair, will suddenly calm,
Because God is the one,
Who can understand.

THE WEATHER

The wind is howling
The lightning is bright.
The thunder is rolling,
It is dark outside.
We complained so much,
When the winter was cold.
There seemed to be,
no end to the snow.
Each season is different,
We can't help but complain
Whether it is cold or hot,
Or there's freezing rain,
I have to admit, autumn is
the best of all.
The leaves change their color,
Before they start to fall.
We need each season,
That comes around,
The winter has a purpose,
It prepares the ground.
For the beautiful gardens,
And all the plants to grow.
So next time we complain,
If the snow begins to fall,
Remember it's the most,
It's the most important season of all.

THE SOLDIER

A soldier knows the danger he faces,
When a war is raging on.
He has no time to think of family,
Who is waiting for him at home.
When night time falls, and he's laying awake,
He is just his mother's son.
He prays for strength and courage,
Until the battle, is won,
he is fighting for the freedom,
Of his country, and fellow man.
He knew he had to do his part,
He had to take a stand,
Many a soldier, have paid a price,
Defending our freedom, and right to live,
Let us remember all the brave young men,
Who gave all they had to give.

The Swinging Bridge

I wish the swinging bridges,
Could still be around today.
They're becoming just a memory,
As things change, along the way.
My favorite memory, of the bridges,
Was watching the debris flow by,
When the floods, came rolling down the river,
After the storms pass by.
The waters made a roaring sound,
As it travelled down the stream.
I'd love to stand there,once again,
To hear the sounds, and dream.
The scariest thing, I can recall,
Was the way the bridge would shake,
When the boys would try to rock it,
With each step that would take.
I hope the few remaining bridges,
Will stay around for awhile,
Each time I return to Kentucky,
I look at them, and smile.

THE TIN ROOF

Pitter Patter, goes the rain drops,
Falling on the old tin roof.
What a peaceful sound it's making,
My soul, it always soothes.
Aah, just to hear that sound once more,
In the cabin with family I loved.
It's just another fond memory,
I know they're looking down, from above.
God has always been good to me,
He helps me make it through,
By letting me recall the good times,
Though I may shed a tear or two.
The tin roof is just a remembrance,
Of my life while I was at home.
I'll take my memories with me,
Wherever I choose to roam.

TRAGEDY ON A MARCH DAY

On a cool and windy march morning,
My husband said to me,
let's go over to my aunt's house,
So I can cut down the tree.
I thought nothing of it, I said okay,
Little did I know, it would be a tragic day.
I made some food to eat later,
After the tree was cut down,
He said,I'll be back in twenty minutes,
He smiled, then he turned around.
I could hear the chain saw running,
I didn't have any doubt,
He knew what he was doing, he had
already figured it out.
His aunt and I sat waiting, for him
to come back in,
After nearly thirty five minutes,
She said, you should check on him.
I walked outside and called his name,
Three, or four times, maybe more.
I thought that he had fallen asleep,
As he had, many times before.
So I walking to the tree,
on the freshly mowed ground.

I looked for him, and called his name,
He was nowhere to be found.
I thought, okay I know he's done.
He just took a different route,
I turned to go, and what I saw, made
me begin to shout.
My heart was beating, so loudly,
I could barely hear myself,
My only thought was running, to
the phone to call for help.
Even though it was a very large tree,
I still couldn't help but think,
That he was going to be okay,
The rescuers face, made my heart sink.
So on this cool and windy march morning
God decided to ease the pain,
He is in a better place now,
There's peace and comfort again.

True Love

I went shopping,the other day,
For some older used poetry books,
I saw one that caught my eye,
So I opened it to take a look.
Written inside the front cover,
Was a message that touched my heart.
I felt almost guilty to read it.
But I knew I had to start.
It said, My dearest Louise, please accept this book,
And come walk with me for awhile.
Let's take a stroll down remembrance Lane,
And the next lines made me smile.
He said, To me you're still that
beautiful young girl,
That you were when we first met.
You've stuck with me through thick and thin,
And we're not finished yet.
I'll hold onto this book, for the rest of my life,
I'll read, and cherish it everyday.
It's been a very long time now,
They both have passed away.

TWO LITTLE DUCKIES

Two little duckies
Swam out on the lake
The first little duckie
Said for goodness sake
My legs are tired
I can't go on
The second little duckie
Said you must be strong
Hop on my back
I'll take you ashore
The first duckie said
Thank you
The second duckie said
What are friends for

Waiting For Spring

My clothes are getting tighter,
My tummy is growing fast.
The weather is really chilly,
How much longer can winter last?
I have a limited income,
New clothes, I cannot buy.
I need to walk away the pounds,
My fat is getting hard to hide.
If we ever return to warm weather,
I promise never to complain.
When the sun starts beating down on me,
I'll try to ignore the pain.
The only thing scary about warm weather,
Is the snakes are going to crawl.
We have bees, and ants, and spiders,
And the tornados will frighten us all.
We will always gripe about the weather.
It's just a part of life,
Winter, summer, spring or fall.
Our disappointment, we cannot hide.

WAITING FOR THE CHANGING

We waited, and waited for warm weather,
It seemed winter would never end.
Then summer arrived with a vengeance,
Now storms are raging again.
There's good and bad with every season,
Though my favorite one of all,
Is the springtime when everythings in bloom,
The beautiful leaves, and coolness,of the fall.
Every season is a gift from our maker,
But it's human nature to complain,
Whether it's cold, and snowy,and freezing,
Or when it seems there's no end to the rain.
Before you know it, winter is back,
We start complaining, all over again.
So let's enjoy the flowers, and the fruit and the sun,
We will be back, again, where we've already been.

Waterfalls

There's something about a waterfall,
That makes you feel at ease.
The sound of the rushingwater.
Can fill your soul with peace.
We had a special waterfall,
Where I lived as a child.
Our creek had a slated bottom,
That went on and on for a mile.
We didn't have the convenience,
Of having water inside,
On laundry day, we all complained,
Our displeasure, we could not hide.
Those buckets, got really heavy,
When the laundry needed to be done.
When we were children we only wanted,
To use the creek for fun.

WHAT DO I WANT FOR CHRISTMAS

I want the knowledge to understand,
The loneliness that eats at me.
I want to be a stronger person,
To deal with,what comes to be.
I want to be a child again,
To erase all of my fears.
Maybe for Christmas I could have,
Laughter, instead of tears.
I want to see better days,
On this troubled road of life.
Then I could have some comfort,
And get rid of all my strife,
for Christmas I will ask God to please,
Take care of those I love.
The ones I still have with me,
And the ones, in heaven above.

What Is A Mother?

A mother is someone who loves you,
With all her heart and soul.
Someone who's love never waivers
Through mistakes we make as we grow.
Someone who thinks, not of herself,
As she comforts you, through your fears,
Whose always ready, with open arms,
As she wipes away your tears.
A mother puts her needs aside,
And rocks you through the night.
She sings you lullabies for comfort.
As she holds you to her chest, so tight.
The years that pass, will never change,
The love of a mother, for a child.
Take time out on Mother's Day,
And show her your love,for a while.
Thank her for the many times,
She gave you all she had to give.
The day will come, when she will be gone,
Let her see your love, while she lives.

WHAT IS MOTHER'S DAY

The day we show appreciation,
To the one who gave us life.
The one who did the best she could,
To teach us wrong from right.
The one who rocked us all night long,
When we were feeling ill.
Who sang us some sweet lullabies,
I can hear her singing,still.
Being a mother is never easy,
When you're a mother you understand.
What I wouldn't give to see my mother,
To hold her well worn hands.
I would hug her, and say thank you mom,
For taking good care of me,
I hope it showed how much I loved you,
I didn't say it, but I hope you could see.

When I Was But A Simple Kid

Where oh where does time go,
It seems like only yesterday,
When off to school I'd go.
Down the hill and up the tracks,
We'd stay seven hours, and then walk back.
Down the track and up the hill,
I wish that I could do it still.
Life was so much simpler back then.
So I thought I'd just pick up a pen,
to jot down, some of the things we did.
When I was but a simple kid.
Going in the woods, swinging on vines,
Playing in the creek, we had good times,
There were no toys, we made our own.
We had no television, we had no phone.
Times have changed in lots of ways,
I'll always remember, the early days,
Nothing ever stays the same,
Let us just be content,
that's the name of the game.

WHEN LIGHT TURNS TO DARK

Sometimes, on your brightest day,
When everything is clear.
The clouds roll in,and steal the light,
And darkness, always appears.
Hold onto the knowledge,
the clouds will leave,
The blue skies will return once more.
You will be wrapped, in a
blanket of sunshine,
Where you'll feel safe and secure,
as before.

WHERE IS HOME

I visited my old homeplace,
it was a shock to me.
The only thing left standing,
was the old stone chimney.
The place is filled with good memories,
And some were bad, I admit,
Now there's weeds and bushes,
where the old home, used to sit.
It was just a four room cabin,
where my grandparents, use to live,
I know I can't go back anymore.
But, oh,what I would give,
To be able to be a child once more,
To go back homeland play,
With all my brothers, and sisters
though most have passed away.
We can remember our home,
with laughs and smiles,
As we look back on our past.
It is still a happy time for me,
I can make my memories last.

WILD FOODS WE ATE

Growing up in the kentucky mountains,
We sampled a lot of wild treats.
Not all of them were pleasant,
Though most of them, were oh so sweet.
Do you remember eating dew berries?
The vine grew low on the ground.
I think it had the sweetest taste,
Of all the berries I found.
walking up the railroad tracks,
On the way to my country school,
I ate my share of the berries,
They were cool from the morning dew.
We ate a lot of different things,
Like sour grassland mountain tea,
The most delicious taste,I recall,
Was the mulberry, and paw-paw tree.
Black walnut, hickory, and beech nuts,
And tea from the sassafrass root,
With all these amazing wild treats,
We were seldom short of food.

Winter

Summer came, and summer went,
I think I'll hibernate.
Winter is not the season for me,
Cold snow I really hate
We complain about hot, we complain about cold,
We can never be satisfied.
I wish it could be spring all year,
Then I wouldn't have to hide,
Underneath all these coats and hats,
Maybe I'll just stay inside.
They say extra pounds,
can keep you warm,
I don't believe that tale is true.
I'm just as cold at a hundred and fifty,
As I was at a hundred and two.
Oh well, I guess I should be happy,
At least I'm still around.
To be able to feel the hot and cold,
I could be six feet underground.

WORKING IN THE MINES

Down under the mountain,
In a deep dark hole
the miners are a laboring,
Digging in the coal.
They cannot be concerned
about the danger they face.
They will make it back out,
If it be by Gods grace.
With a prayer on their lips,
They keep shoveling the coal,
The dust on their lungs,
Will one day take a toll.
Many miners are injured,
When the mine caves in.
it doesn't stop the miner,
He will return once again.
At home the family waits,
As the hours drag slowly on,
They knew in their heart,
In a flash he could be gone.
Thank God for the coal miner,
Who put their lives on the line.
They keep their family from hunger,
By digging in the mine.

Worshipping

When I left for church this morning,
I was feeling, oh so good.
The sermon was great,as usual.
As only a great pastor could.
The pastor then said to us all,
When you leave this church today,
your worshipping should continue,
At home, and in other ways.
Well that I certainly understood,
it made good sense to me.
But then he told us something else.
And I thought, oh no!, that can't be!
he said, God doesn't hear your prayers,
If you're holding onto a grudge.
So I have to start all over,
And stop trying to be a judge.
I love God with all my heart,
I'll stop judging my fellow men,
I'll toss aside my resentment because,
I don't need another sin.

YARD SAILING

Warm weather has arrived at last,
Yard sales are being arranged.
It's time to take out my collection,
And sell it for mere change.
It makes no difference, how low the price,
It's just never low enough.
Of course we agree, to make a deal,
We're trying to unload this (stuff)
Packing it all back up again,
Is something we hate to do
Shoppers already know these things.
That's why they bargain with you.
At the end of the long hot day,
After we count up all our change,
We have made enough, to buy more things,
So another sale can be arranged.
It's really a vicious cycle,
We just can't help ourselves,
Next time when I have my sale,
I'll say, pay my price, or go
somewhere else!

Yesterday Is Gone

It does not make any difference,
To go back in time and say,
If I had done things different,
Would I be any happier today?
I think there's not any reason,
To fret about what could have been.
The answers are nowhere to be found,
They are blowing in the wind.
WE make choices, much too quickly,
Searching for that elusive dream.
Worry not, about your yesterdays,
They have to stay, where they've always been.
When you are laying alone in the darkness,
The grief can consume your soul.
hang onto the thought,the light will appear,
you still have a ways to go.

THE FRAIL LITTLE WOMAN AND UNBORN CHILD

Back in 19 and 51, late October with a setting sun.
With snow on the ground, and kids having fun,'
A frail little woman, with a heart so kind.
Was trying to give birth, to child number nine.
Life was never easy, in these mountains of boughs,
Her life had been hard, her body did show.
Her labor was hard, and her body was frail
To last through the night, no one could tell.
They all gave up hope, nothing more could be done.
For this frail little woman, and her unborn one.
Please don't let me go, hold onto my hand.
There's still life in me, you must understand.
There's so much more, in life I must do.
Like raising my child, that I'm giving birth to.
The doctors all knew, no way she would last.'
She would die before dawn, she was failing fast.
While still on the gurney, she was rolled through the door.
To die in the hallway, on the hospital floor.
With no gown on her body, only covered with a sheet.
And soon to be found, in eternal sleep.
Please don't let me go, hold onto my hand,
There's still life in me, you must understand.
There's so much more, in life I must do
Like raising my child, I'm giving birth to.

Death would be calling, to open the door
For the frail little woman, and the child that she bore
But as time went by, and all through the night,
The frail little woman, would find courage to fight.
Death had come near, but then passed her by.
Death saw the light, and twinkle in her eye
The frail little woman, gave birth to a son
She held onto her life, and as both they were one.
Please don't let me go, hold onto my hand
There's still life in me, you must understand.
There's so much more in life, that I must do
Like raising my child, I'm giving birth to.
The morning had come, the sun was at high
When the doctors came through, and passed her by
A baby was crying, so they looked and then smiled
At the frail little woman, and her newborn child
Her will to live, was all that she had
It was plenty enough, so this story's not sad.
Now the frail little woman, and her child would sleep
Could this story be true, and what would you think
This story won't end, and the child would grow
This story of wonders, now has been told
For I was the child, the frail woman did hold.
When times get so bad, you can always find,
As long as there's hope, you'll have peace of mind
Don't ever give up, if there's death at your door
Hold onto your life, just a little bit more
When all else is said, and all has been done.
Only then will you find, the fight has been won.
So I give you my story, of my mother so frail
Of the hardships she had, and she did not fail
Hold onto your soul, in it there's life
Then you can face, the darkness of night

By Ivan Stewart

www.ingramcontent.com/pod-product-compliance
Ingram Content Group UK Ltd.
Pitfield, Milton Keynes, MK11 3LW, UK
UKHW041944190726
13854UKWH00004B/1778